THE HUMAN BODY

THE DIGESTIVE SYSTEM

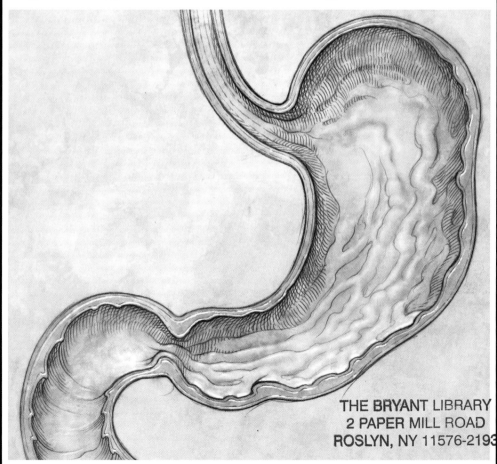

By Susan H. Gray

The
Child's World

Published in the United States of America by the Child's World®
P.O. Box 326, Chanhassen, MN 55317-0326
800-599-READ
www.childsworld.com

Subject adviser:
R. John Solaro, Ph.D.,
Distinguished
University Professor
and Head, Department
of Physiology and
Biophysics, University
of Illinois Chicago,
Chicago, Illinois

Photo Credits: Cover: Artville/Scott Bodell; Bettmann/Corbis:15; Corbis: 4 (Mark E. Gibson), 9 (LWA-Stephen Welstead), 14 (Howard Sochurek), 17 (Richard T. Nowitz), 20 (Ed Bock), 22 (Jim Cummins); Custom Medical Stock Pictures: 7, 8, 10, 12, 13, 16, 18, 19, 23, 25; PhotoEdit: 21 (Bill Aron), 24 (Tim McCarthy), 26 (Mark Richards), 27 (Michael Newman).

The Child's World®: Mary Berendes, Publishing Director

Editorial Directions, Inc.: E. Russell Primm, Editorial Director; Elizabeth K. Martin, Line Editor; Katie Marsico, Assistant Editor; Olivia Nellums, Editorial Assistant; Susan Hindman, Copy Editor; Elizabeth K. Martin, Proofreader; Peter Garnham, Marilyn Mallin, Mary Hoffman, Fact Checkers; Tim Griffin/IndexServ, Indexer; Cian Loughlin O'Day, Photo Researcher; Linda S. Koutris, Photo Selector

Library of Congress Cataloging-in-Publication Data
Gray, Susan Heinrichs.
 The digestive system / by Susan H. Gray.
  p. cm. — (Living well)
Includes bibliographical references and index.
Contents: What is the digestive system?—What happens in the mouth?—What happens in the stomach?—What happens in the small intestine?—What about the large intestine?
 ISBN 1-59296-037-5 (lib. bdg. : alk. paper)
 1. Digestive organs—Juvenile literature. [1. Digestive system.] I. Title. II. Series: Living well (Child's World (Firm)
 QP145.G687 2004
 612.3—dc21   2003006289

TABLE OF CONTENTS

CHAPTER ONE

NEVER AGAIN

Tony and his friends were eating lunch together under an

oak tree. Today was the class picnic, and the food was

*As Tony ate, his digestive system was hard at work breaking
down the food into things his body could use.*

great. Tony had two hot dogs and a pile of potato chips. He downed three glasses of lemonade. The picnic was not over yet, and Tony was already stuffed. Then his teacher brought out a plate of cupcakes.

Tony groaned. He loved cupcakes. But he just could not eat another thing. He leaned back against the tree and closed his eyes. He slid his hand over his stomach. It felt round and tight. Inside, his stomach had stretched as far as it could. It was working hard to deal with all the food that Tony had eaten. Special fluids were coming from his stomach's inner walls. The fluids were mixing with the hot dogs and buns. They were blending in with the potato chips. The fluids began slowly breaking everything down.

Tony did not care what happened in his stomach. He just knew he had eaten way too much. He groaned a second time and sighed, "I'll never do that again."

CHAPTER TWO

WHAT IS THE DIGESTIVE SYSTEM?

T o digest something means to break it down. The digestive system is the group of organs that break down and absorb food.

The main organs of this system are hollow and joined end-to-end, like a tube. The mouth is the first part of the digestive system. Next comes the esophagus (ee-SOFF-uh-gus), which leads to the stomach. The intestines make up the last part of this system. Sometimes the stomach and intestines together are called the gut.

Two other organs are also involved in digestion. These are the liver and pancreas (PAN-kree-us). They are not part of the tube, but they are nearby. They make the juices that help digest food.

One job of the digestive system is to change food into materials the body can use. The body cannot use meat, bread, or most other foods as they are. These foods are made of **molecules** that are too large to be useful to the body. So the digestive system breaks them down into smaller and smaller molecules. The body

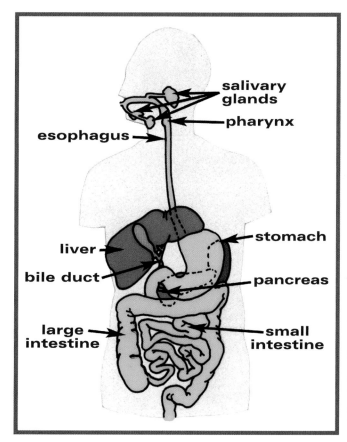

As food passes through the different organs of the digestive system, it gets broken down more and more and its nutrients are absorbed into the body.

uses these **nutrients** for all of its normal activities.

Another job of the digestive system is to get those nutrients into the bloodstream. Then the blood can carry them all through the body. The nutrients travel to places where the body can use them.

The inside of the digestive system is wet and slippery. This is

because of the many glands lining it. Digestive glands are little bundles of cells that produce fluids. Some glands of the digestive system produce fluids that keep the food moist. Some produce liquids that help break down the food.

These cells line the inside of the stomach.

The walls of the tube have blood vessels and nerves in them. They also have muscles. The muscles squeeze and relax, making the digestive organs move. You cannot feel your stomach or intestines move. But sometimes you can hear sounds coming from them. They are quite busy, especially after a meal. Their movements push food through the tube.

CHAPTER THREE

WHAT HAPPENS
IN THE MOUTH?

The digestive system starts with the mouth. This is where food first comes into the body. Teeth bite off pieces of food. The teeth in the front of the mouth are sharp. They are made for biting and tearing food. The teeth in the back of the mouth are wide and are made for

Teeth are the first part of the digestive system. They will help make this sandwich into smaller pieces.

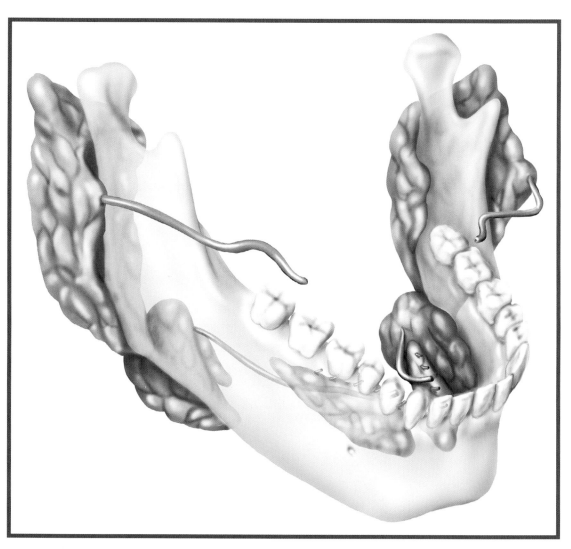

Three pairs of salivary glands in the mouth help to break down food and make it moist.

chewing. These back teeth grind food into smaller and smaller

bits. The tongue shoves food this way and that, helping the teeth

to chew everything. Little bumps on the tongue are lined with taste buds. These detect the different flavors of food as it is being chewed.

Salivary (SAL-ih-VEHR-ee) glands go to work as soon as food enters the mouth. These glands make saliva, or spit. Three pairs of glands release saliva into the mouth. The first pair is in the cheeks, one on either side of the mouth, right in front of the ears. The other two pairs lie within the lower jaw. Little tubes run from the glands and open into the mouth. Saliva from the glands makes the food moist. It also starts breaking down some foods into smaller molecules. When a person is nervous, chemicals are released to stop the flow of saliva. That makes the mouth feel dry.

Once food is ground up, the tongue shoves it to the back of the mouth. Muscles in this area squeeze together. They push food into the throat. As food starts down the throat, a little flap called

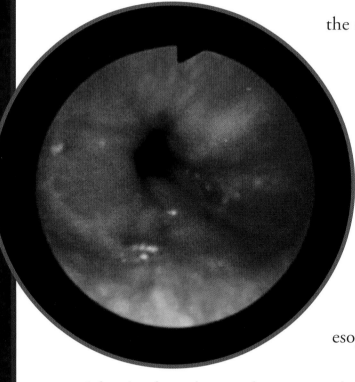

A doctor's endoscope lets us see the muscular walls of the esophagus.

the epiglottis (EP-ih-GLOT-iss) acts. It flops over and covers the opening of the windpipe. This keeps food from going into the lungs.

Food moves down the esophagus. This is the tube running from the back of the mouth down to the stomach. Glands in the esophagus walls add fluid as the food moves by. Food does not just fall to the stomach by gravity. The esophagus has muscular walls. These muscles gently squeeze and relax, moving food on to the stomach.

CHAPTER FOUR

WHAT HAPPENS IN THE STOMACH?

The stomach is a little like a bag. It is hollow and shaped like the letter J. Inside, it is moist and wrinkled. Like the esophagus, its walls are made of muscle tissue. When food enters, the muscles relax for a bit. This lets the stomach stretch out to hold that food.

Cells in the stomach wall make fluids that mix with the food. Some cells let out fluids that break down meat. Some cells let out fluids that break down fats. Some cells produce a strong acid. Other cells produce mucus (MYOO-kuss). Mucus coats the inside of the stomach. It protects the stomach lining, especially from the acid.

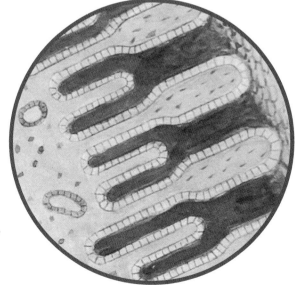

Folds in the stomach's lining help it make fluids and break down food.

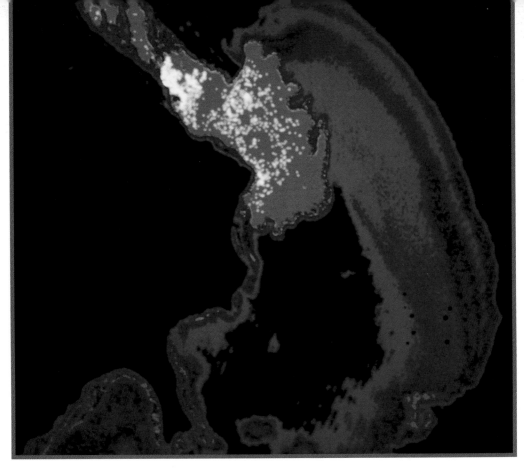

*This electronic scan shows food entering the stomach
from the esophagus to be turned into chyme.*

After food comes in, the stomach goes to work. The muscular

walls squeeze and relax, pushing the food around. The cells release

their fluids. Food becomes covered with acid and mucus. It mixes up

with fluids that break it down into smaller molecules. When the stom-

ach is done with it, food is wet and mushy. This mushy material is

called chyme (KIME).

The year was 1822. William Beaumont (BO-mont) was working as an army doctor. One day he was called to the scene of an accident. A young trapper named Alexis St. Martin had suffered a terrible wound. A gun had gone off by mistake and blown part of his stomach away.

Beaumont worked tirelessly on the young man (right). Despite all his work, Beaumont feared Alexis would be dead within days.

Instead, the young man began to heal. However, the hole over his stomach never closed completely. A small opening remained. Through this hole, Beaumont could see inside the man's stomach.

Over the years, Beaumont continued to work with Alexis. He watched what happened to different foods in the stomach. He collected juices from the man's stomach and sent them to other scientists. In 1833, Beaumont wrote a book about the things he had learned. Beaumont's book made it clear that the stomach used chemicals to break down food.

Dr. Beaumont became famous for his work. Alexis St. Martin went on with his life. He got married and had kids. His stomach never healed, but that did not seem to slow him down. Alexis died in his 80s. He had lived with that hole for more than 60 years.

CHAPTER FIVE

WHAT HAPPENS IN THE SMALL INTESTINE?

Chyme moves out of the stomach and right into the small intestine. This is a folded and twisted tube that is about 20 feet (6.1 meters) long in an adult. Not far from the intestines are three other important organs. These are the pancreas, the liver, and the gall bladder. Little tubes run from these organs into the small intestine. Fluids from the organs go through the tubes. They mix with food that enters the intestine.

Fluid from the pancreas breaks down **proteins** (PRO-teenz), **fats,** and **carbohydrates** (KAR-bo-HY-drates).

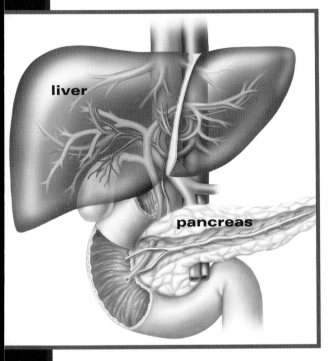

The pancreas and liver create fluids to aid the small intestine.

The gall bladder helps break down fatty foods, such as a hamburger.

It also weakens the strong acid from the stomach. Fluid from the liver

goes into the gall bladder. From there, it flows into the small intestine.

This fluid is called bile. It helps the small intestine work on fats. After

someone eats a fatty meal, the gall bladder goes into action. It squeezes

out its bile, sending it into the small intestine.

The small intestine breaks down most food so that the body can absorb its nutrients. The large food molecules are broken down into smaller and smaller pieces. Another important thing happens in the small intestine. The food is absorbed. The molecules are now small enough to seep into the intestine's walls. Tiny blood vessels in the walls pick up these nutrients. Once they enter the blood, they are sent throughout the body.

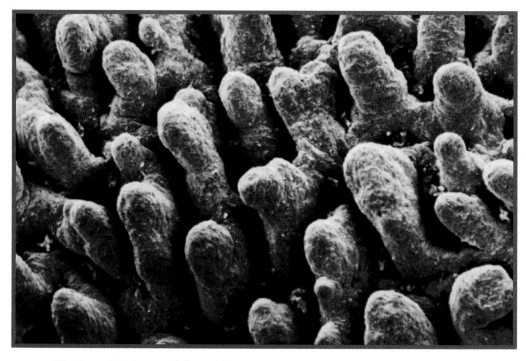

The fingerlike lining of the small intestines (called villi) helps absorb nutrients.

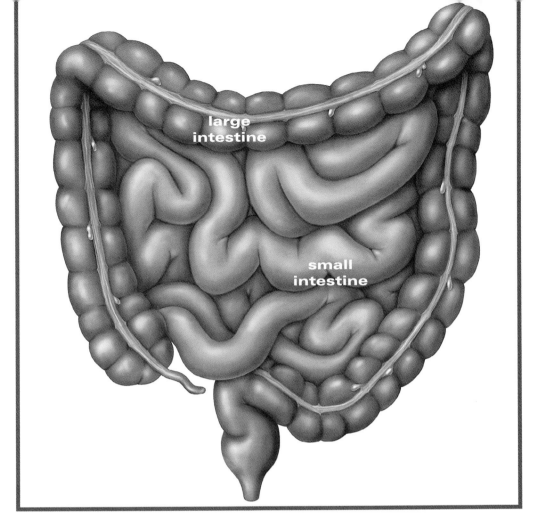

*It takes a long time for food to move through the many folds
of the small intestine into the large intestine.*

Food takes hours to move through the small intestine. It travels

through all the curves and kinks and bends. Movements of the intes-

tine shove the food along. Muscles in the intestine walls squeeze and

relax. They do this in a wave of motion. The wave of muscle action

slowly propels food forward.

Most of the food we eat falls into three main groups. These groups are proteins, fats, and carbohydrates (sometimes called carbs). Meat, fish, eggs, and cheese are loaded with proteins. A protein is a huge molecule. It gets broken down in the digestive system into smaller molecules. The body can use these smaller molecules for growth, to build cells, and for energy. The muscles and nerves also need protein to work properly.

The body needs fat molecules, too. These are found in foods such as butter and oil. The body uses fat for energy. It also needs fat to build cells.

A fatty material covers the nerve cells and helps them work the way they should.

Carbohydrates are the third main group. Carbohydrate molecules are found in bread, pasta, potatoes, cereal, and corn. They give the body energy. The body needs energy even when it seems to be doing nothing. When people are at rest, their muscles are at work holding the body in place. Nerves are working away in the brain. Lungs are taking in air. The heart is pumping. All of these activities need energy. Much of that energy comes from carbohydrates.

CHAPTER SIX

WHAT ABOUT THE LARGE INTESTINE?

After several hours, food finally reaches the end of the small intestine. By now, most proteins, fats, and carbohydrates have been broken down into small molecules. Most of these molecules have been drawn into the bloodstream. These are many of the nutrients that the body needs to work.

In a few hours, what's left of these egg rolls will reach the large intestine.

The food that is left over moves into the large intestine. The large

intestine is actually shorter than the small intestine. In an adult, it is

around 5 feet (1.5 meters) long. The large intestine starts on the right

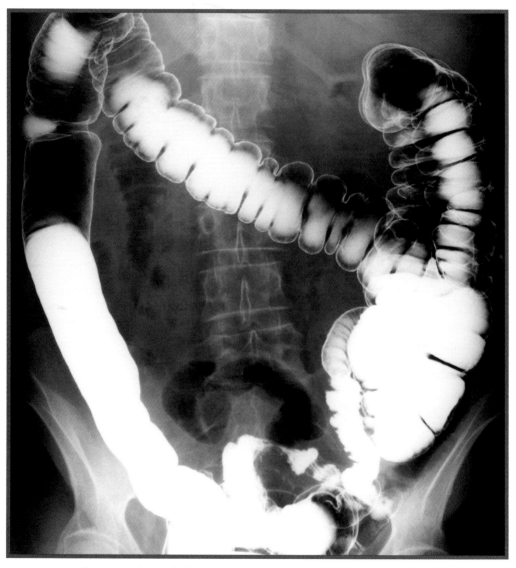

This X ray shows the large intestine as it curves around the abdomen.

side of the body, not far from

the belly button. From there,

it runs straight up and across

to the left side. Then it runs

back down and out of the body.

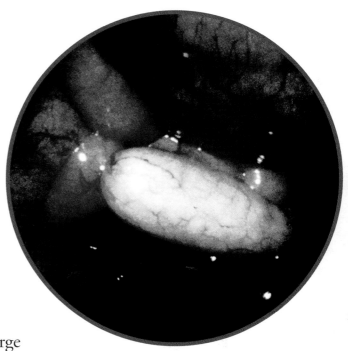

The appendix looks like a finger branching off the large intestine.

Like the other organs, the large

intestine also has muscular walls. As

the walls move, they push the leftover food forward and sometimes

backward. As food is pushed about, water and salts are removed from

it. These are drawn through the intestinal walls and into the blood, to

be used by the body. In time, the remaining food wastes pass out of

the body.

One tiny organ lies near the start of the large intestine. This is the

appendix. It looks like a little finger. No one knows exactly what it

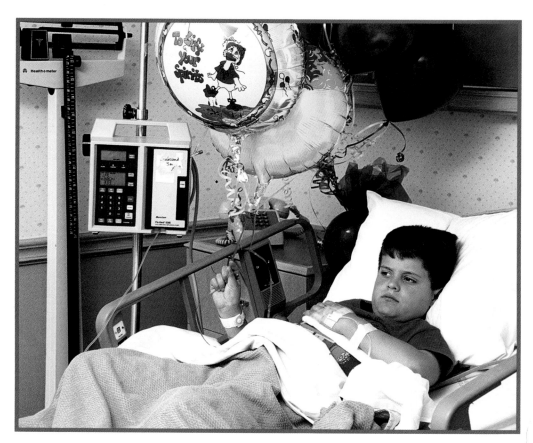

The appendix can become infected and cause a lot of pain near your stomach. When this happens, a doctor can remove the appendix through surgery.

does. Sometimes, though, it becomes diseased. Doctors are not always

sure why this happens. It may happen when the digestive system is

infected. The condition is called appendicitis (uh-PEN-duh-SY-tiss). A

person with appendicitis feels terrible pain in the right side. A doctor

must remove the diseased appendix. Otherwise, it may burst, causing

even more trouble.

CHAPTER SEVEN

WHY DO YOU GET AN UPSET STOMACH?

Appendicitis is not the only problem people have with the system. Sometimes bacteria or viruses get in and cause sickness. These germs enter when someone takes in impure water or food. The germs can give a person an upset stomach or make the intestines hurt. They might even cause nausea (NAW-zee-uh), which is a queasy feeling. Or worse, they might make a person throw up. Usually, the body gets over this in a day or two.

Motion sickness can also disturb the digestive system. This is a feeling of nausea people get when they ride in a car or on a boat or plane. Sometimes they say they get

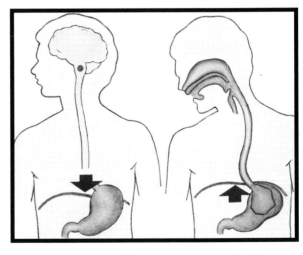

Sometimes germs will cause your stomach to become upset. Your brain will then send a signal to the stomach and tell it to throw up any food inside.

Riding in a car can confuse your brain and make you feel queasy.

carsick or airsick. Germs do not cause the illness. It occurs when the

brain cannot sort out all of the signals coming to it. Suppose you are

standing on the deck of a boat. Your eyes can see that you are moving

forward. But signals from the leg muscles tell your brain that you are

standing still. Organs in your ear know that the boat is rocking and

you are losing your balance. But nerves in your feet tell the brain that

you are standing firm. The brain cannot make sense of all these sig-

The digestive system allows us to enjoy delicious meals and keeps our bodies healthy.

nals. When the brain gets confused like this, a person begins to feel dizzy. The stomach tightens up. The person might even sweat heavily and throw up.

Usually, the digestive system does not have such problems. It works day and night, breaking down the food we eat and moving it on. It takes care of big meals when we overeat. It handles little snacks. It prepares food to be used by every cell in the body.

Glossary

absorb (ab-ZORB) To absorb something is to soak it up.

carbohydrates (KAR-bo-HY-drates) Carbohydrates are materials found in sugary or starchy foods.

fats (FATZ) Fats are materials found in oily or greasy foods.

molecules (MOL-uh-kyoolz) Molecules are extremely small parts of something.

nutrients (NOO-tree-uhnts) Nutrients are the things found in foods needed for life and health.

proteins (PROH-teenz) Proteins are materials found in meat, fish, eggs, dairy products, and some other foods.

Questions and Answers about the Digestive System

How long does food stay in the stomach? Your stomach usually takes three to four hours to do its part digesting food.

Do some foods take longer than others to digest? Greasy and fatty foods are harder for your digestive system to handle, so they take longer to digest.

What kinds of food help the digestive system? Foods with a lot of fiber, such as bread, cereal, fruits, and vegetables, all help your digestive system do its job. Drinking plenty of water also helps.

What is an ulcer? An ulcer is a painful sore or hole in the lining of the stomach. Doctors once believed that spicy food and stress led to ulcers. They now believe ulcers are caused by a certain kind of bacteria. Today, there are many medications that can treat ulcers.

Did You Know?

- In William Beaumont's time, some doctors believed that the stomach ground up food. Others thought the stomach cooked it.

- The whole digestive system in an adult is about 25 to 30 feet (7.6 to 9 meters) long.

- Cows, sheep, and goats have stomachs with several chambers. These animals swallow grass, which goes into one chamber. Then it comes back up, and they chew it again. The grass then goes to the other chambers, where it is digested.

- Bumps on the tongue come in several different shapes. If you stick your tongue out and look at its very back, you will see a few large, round bumps.

- Sometimes people have a pain they call heartburn. But it has nothing to do with the heart. It is really caused by stomach acid coming up into the esophagus.

How to Learn More about the Digestive System

At the Library

Silverstein, Alvin, Virginia Silverstein, and Robert Silverstein.
The Digestive System.
New York: Twenty-First Century Books, 1997.

Stille, Darlene R.
The Digestive System.
Danbury, Conn.: Children's Press, 1997.

Walker, Pam, and Elaine Wood.
The Digestive System.
San Diego: Lucent Books, 2003.

On the Web

Visit our home page for lots of links about the digestive system:
http://www.childsworld.com/links.html
Note to Parents, Teachers, and Librarians: We routinely verify our
Web links to make sure they're safe, active sites—so encourage
your readers to check them out!

Through the Mail or by Phone

AMERICAN GASTROENTEROLOGICAL ASSOCIATION

4930 Del Ray Avenue

Bethesda, MD 20814

301-654-2055

http://www.gastro.org

NATIONAL INSTITUTE OF DIABETES
AND DIGESTIVE AND KIDNEY DISEASES

National Institutes of Health

Office of Communications and Public Liaison

Building 31, Room 9A04

Center Drive, MSC 2560

Bethesda, MD 20892-2560

http://www.niddk.nih.gov

Index

About the Author

Susan H. Gray has a bachelor's and a master's degree in zoology, and has taught college-level anatomy and physiology courses. In her 25 years as an author, she has written many medical articles, grant proposals, and children's books. Ms. Gray enjoys gardening, traveling, and playing the piano and organ. She has traveled twice to the Russian Far East to give organ workshops to church musicians. She also works extensively with American and Russian friends to develop medical and social service programs for Vladivostok, Russia. Ms. Gray and her husband, Michael, live in Cabot, Arkansas.